A Rubric for Transition Among Cultures

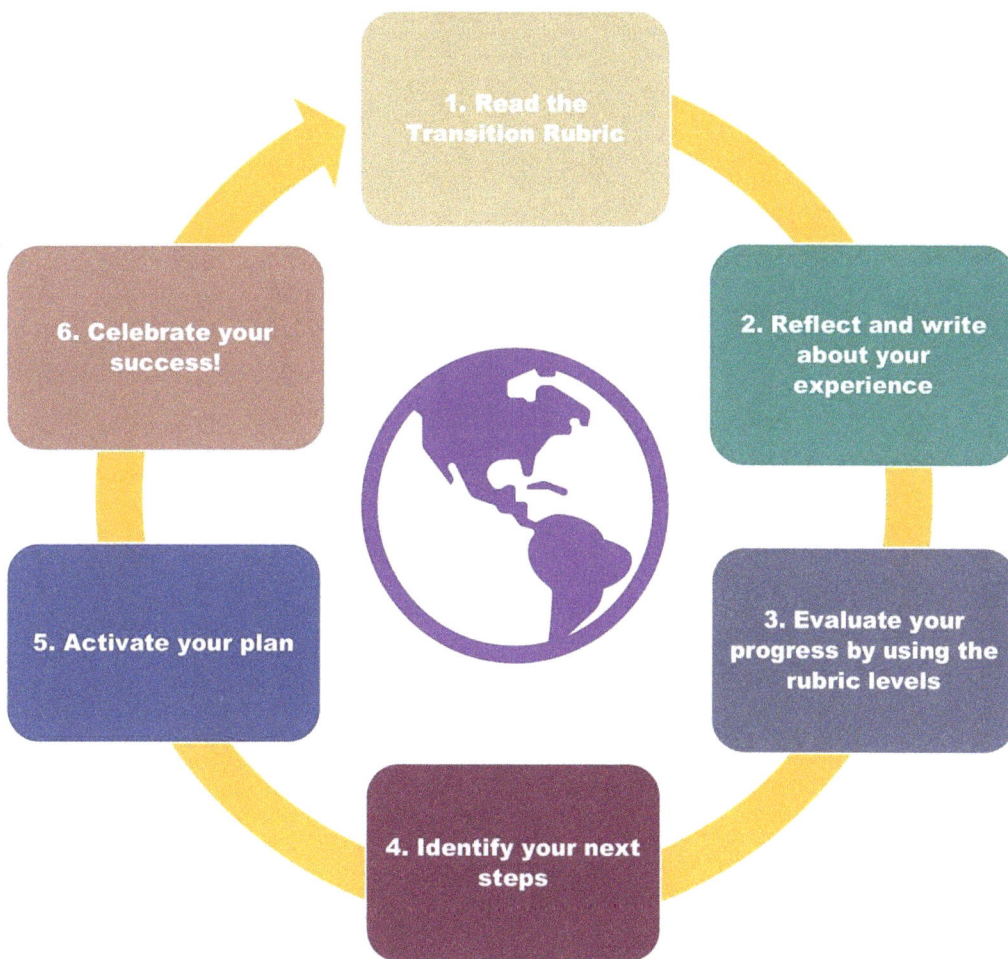

1. Read the Transition Rubric

2. Reflect and write about your experience

3. Evaluate your progress by using the rubric levels

4. Identify your next steps

5. Activate your plan

6. Celebrate your success!

To Assist and Inform Cross-culture Transition Progress

Rachel E. Timmons, Ed.D.

Praise for A Rubric for Transition Among Cultures

I grew up in India as a Missionary Kid where I attended a boarding school as a child. I traveled back and forth between India and the USA many times as a child and later in my adult years. I also taught in the Woodstock high school in the Himalayas for several years. However, I first learned about being a Third Culture Person from my colleague Dr. Timmons while collaborating on course development for courses in International Education. Dr. Timmons' Reacculturation Rubric was a fine addition to the Cross-culture Competence Course content. I also led six International Service Project groups of students to Asia and I found the Reacculturation Rubric to be useful for the discussions and debriefing after each trip.

Joe DeVol, Retired Missionary and Professor of Education, California Baptist University

As a school psychologist who works with many students who are dealing with acculturation processes and who are Third Culture Students, this work has been extremely helpful in better understanding the needs and issues they may face, as well as recognizing the strengths and assets these students bring from their unique backgrounds and international experiences. Dr. Timmons' Reacculturation Cross-culture Transition Rubric has been an excellent and useful tool in helping the teachers know how to understand, support, encourage, and instruct our multi-cultural students. I have also shared this Reacculturation Rubric with other school psychologists who work at international schools in different countries.

Sarah Pate, School Psychologist in California and Doha, Qatar

As a student in Dr. Timmons' Cross-culture Competence course I have learned so much about what it means to be a TCP. I came to the USA directly from Indonesia with minimum English competency. However, now as a graduate student, I have not only improved in English but I can also help support my friends from other countries as they make cross-cultural adjustments. The Reacculturation Rubric is very informative and helps us see what to do next in our adjustment as international students. This will also help us when we go back to our home countries.

Yuli Susanti, Graduate Student from Indonesia

My sister and I finally got a copy of the Reacculturation Rubric after hearing Dr. Timmons speak about TCKs at a conference. We were both ready to quit college and go back to our host culture until we learned how to take steps to readjust to living in our home culture.

Two College Students (who wish to remain anonymous)

I've gone over so many times the rubric you've sent to me, Rachel, and it is like finally there is something on paper that describes what I've been experiencing in words. Even though it's been almost a year now that I've been home, I feel in many ways like it was yesterday. I don't think I'm much out of your rubric's stage one except for a few areas, but at least I have hope for continuing through the reacculturation process with success.

Christie Nelson, Christian Ministries and ESL Teacher in Thailand and China

This book is dedicated to my daughters Amy, Sarah, Cynthia, and Elizabeth, who have successfully grown up across cultures, to my husband, Bill, who had the vision for our cross-cultural adventures, and to dear friends and colleagues around the world.

You have all provided the support, interest, and encouragement that has enabled me to develop this Reacculturation Cross-culture Transition Rubric.

Contents

Foreword

We prepare ourselves to face stress and difficulties when transitioning to a foreign land. We anticipate everything will be new and different and it will take some time to get used to new customs, value systems, food, climate, and much more. Rarely do we prepare ourselves for the reverse transition. But the experts tell us that repatriation can be just as – if not more – difficult than going abroad: up to three times more difficult.

I can attest to that. When I returned home after living 15 consecutive years abroad with my own family, things had changed while I was away. I had changed in many subtle ways. I had a whole new worldview and found that I appreciated things back home that I had once taken for granted. There were also some things that really irritated me about my home country culture and people. But no one prepared me or my family for any of this.

That's why, when I first met Dr. Rachel Timmons at a Families in Global Transition conference and heard her present on her Reacculturation Rubric, I was so thrilled. Finally, a tool that helps people understand the emotions, challenges, and struggles associated with repatriation.

Through her research, Dr. Timmons has taken an amalgamation of hundreds of years of Third Culture Persons' cross-cultural experiences and developed a tool that can be used to try to understand various facets of life in re-entry transition. While not every category she presents for thought and reflection will be applicable to every individual, the majority force self-reflection on the often-overlooked intangible losses that are so difficult to recognize.

I consider this rubric to be an absolute treasure and feel every person about to experience repatriation should receive a copy. That is why I refer to the Reacculturation Rubric in my book *The Global Nomad's Guide to University Transition* and recommend it to everyone who takes my Training of Trainers course to help Third Culture Kids repatriating for their university experience and/or families facing repatriation. I consider it a key resource and am so pleased Dr. Timmons has decided to turn it into a book for easy access to all.

Tina L. Quick

Author of *The Global Nomad's Guide to University Transition* and *Survive and Thrive: The International Student's Guide to Succeeding in the U.S.*

Introduction

Dear Fellow Sojourner,

My name is Rachel Timmons, and before returning to America, I spent 25 years living in a host culture (10 years in the Philippines and 15 years in Thailand), where my husband and I raised our four children. We taught at international schools during our years abroad, developed adoption and foster care programs, and worked with relief and development services. Living abroad for 25 years and working in a global school setting for most of those years provided the foundation for understanding the specific needs of international students and their families as they learn in a culture that is often different than their passport cultures. It was through this international teaching and cross-cultural experience that I became interested in the area of helping people make healthy cross-culture transitions. This interest led me to research the phenomenology of what it means to be a Third Culture Person (TCP) who can make healthy cross-culture transitions.

During our time in Thailand I met David Pollock. He had a passion for speaking to students and families about cross-culture adjustments and what it means to be a Third Culture Kid (TCK). When he and Ruth Van Reken published their book *Third Culture Kids: The Experience of Growing up Among Worlds*, it became a guide for our family: my teenage children were about to return to the USA, and I was concerned about their adjustment after being raised in Asia from birth to 18. Soon my husband and I followed our children and returned to the USA, where I began teaching at California Baptist University in the School of Education.

Since returning to America, I have served as a professor of education at the university level, and I stay involved with international students and Third Culture People. I continue to research cross-culture transitions and the TCP phenomenon. As a result, I have developed a research-based assessment rubric based on more than *430 years of the combined transition experience of fellow TCP sojourners* to help guide Third Culture People through successful cross-culture transition.

Over time I have realized that beyond international living, many monocultural students and people of all ages regularly experience transitions from one culture to another through their work or school experiences. Transitions from military service to civilian life, from COVID-19 isolation back to regular society or from virtual schooling to face-to-face schooling can pose issues similar to cross-culture transition challenges.

Finally, one could conclude that *all of life seems to be a continual transition,* indicating that we must all become adept at transitioning through each new phase of our lives. Although this Reacculturation Rubric was primarily intended for transitioning in cross-cultural situations, it can also be applied to life transitions in general.

Sojourners, I hope you find this Reacculturation Cross-culture Transition Rubric a helpful guide throughout your life's transitions, whether at home or abroad.

If you have questions or comments, please feel free to contact me at timonsr@sbcglobal.net.

Your fellow sojourner,
Rachel E. Timmons

Reacculturation Transition Explained

Reacculturation is a term associated with cross-culture transition. We are all people shaped and written upon by our surrounding culture, and as we move between different cultures, we must reacculturate ourselves to live happily in each new situation or culture that we may find ourselves in. To reacculturate ourselves during times of transition takes work. It takes effort to motivate oneself to join new groups, make new friends, study new languages, or enjoy new living conditions. Without effort in each reacculturation transition area, a person can stop progressing to competence and may even fossilize or become stuck in a particular area of transition development. This is why a rubric is a helpful tool for assessing transition progress. A rubric lets us recognize our progress and see if we have become stuck and hardened like a rock rather than developing the competencies needed to complete reacculturation in each new cross-cultural experience and in all areas of life.

The following continuum explains the Reacculturation Cross-culture Transition Process.

Reacculturation Transition Journey Continuum Stages

Stage 1: My Current Life of Healthy Acculturation in My Host Culture	Stage 2: Forward Look at Possibilities for Reacculturation and Transition Growth	Stage 3: Active Steps for Reacculturation in My New Culture	Stage 4: Self-Assess Reacculturation Progress
1. Full involvement: make an honest appraisal of your full involvement in your current host or home community.	2. Take a forward look at Reacculturation and involvement possibilities in your next host or home community prior to disengaging from your past culture.	3. Take active steps prior to making your transition to get reinvolved in your new setting. Plan ahead for the bumpy places in your transition by discussing possible areas of *fossilization* with your family and close friends.	4. Use the Reacculturation Rubric to assess your transition progress in your new culture. *Reflect* and *Assess* often to ensure appropriate levels of reinvolvement and healthy transition progress. Take time to enjoy your progress.

Rubrics or Continuums

The meaning of the word rubric (also known as a continuum) has to do with providing directions or guidance on how to manage an assignment or complete a process. Rubrics are commonly used in educational circles to describe the steps, stages, or progress in different areas of academic development.

A rubric or continuum is also used to describe development in other areas of personal life. This Reacculturation Rubric describes the general issues of transitioning from one place to another, thus guiding a person through the transition process into a successful cross-culture transition. Each general area in a rubric has several elements (sections) under the headings that help break down the big ideas of that area into smaller chunks of information so that the reader can get a closer look at themselves as they reflect on their progress in that specific area of transition. Finally, a rubric or continuum serves as a self-assessment strategy for the reader to evaluate their progress on the task or process described in the rubric elements.

Content and Elements of the Reacculturation Transition Rubric

Every rubric has big ideas in the content and several elements associated with the big ideas that the rubric is designed to measure. Each element under the big idea of the rubric content helps break down the ideas into measurable steps. Explaining each content area with detailed descriptors helps the reader understand what the element is measuring. For example, the first content area of the Reacculturation Rubric deals with the *TCP Reacculturation Process*. This content area has four elements that help explain the Reacculturation Transition Process. These elements are as follows: Reverse Culture shock, Cultural Fatigue, Expectations of Home Culture, and Stress or Health Problems. By describing each of these elements in great detail, a person can see where they fit in the reacculturation process and determine their progress in achieving the desired competencies. The second rubric content area is that of *TCP Marginalization*. To be marginalized means that a TCP person is in some way made *less* than they were before as a result of being out of their home country and living in a host culture for an extended time. Marginalization could mean that a student is not prepared academically in the same way as peers in their home country are prepared, so they cannot succeed as well in school as they did before returning to their home country. It could also mean that professionals have to take a pay cut because they have not worked in their home country for the past few years. *Support and Belonging* are also TCP issues that are important to keep in mind when moving among cultures. TCPs leave friends and family to move to different places, and a sense of belonging does not necessarily follow them to each new experience. To belong to a new community takes work, patience, and willingness to try different approaches for meeting new people and fitting into another cultural society. *Cultural Heritage* is the next content area in this rubric. A Third Culture Person builds their sense of self as they grow and develop in the culture surrounding them. Therefore, they have a cultural heritage that becomes part of their identity. When TCPs change their cultural environment, their identity can get confused or somewhat lost as they transition or reacculturate into the next culture. It takes awareness and mental and emotional work to maintain a healthy sense of self when transitioning or reacculturating into a new cultural environment. The area of *TCP Re-entry Preparation* is very important. Sending organizations and international schools can play a vital role in helping returnees prepare for their new life in their new home. TCPs must develop a realistic view of their social and academic preparation for their life transitions and continue to build upon those preparations until their cross-culture transition is complete.

Why Use a Rubric to Help Make a Healthy Cross-culture Transition?

There are three critical reasons why a Third Culture Person should use a Reacculturation Transition Rubric. The first is to *Develop Cross-cultural Competence*. Just as students develop necessary skills for succeeding in school and in academic areas, people in cross-culture transition must develop cross-cultural competence quickly in each new cultural situation. For example, students entering college must develop the ability to function effectively and efficiently in their new home and school community. A rubric simply acts as a guide to help a person make good decisions and to see their progress concerning readjustment in their new school and cultural environment. The second reason to use a Reacculturation Transition Rubric is to *Develop a Sense of Self-efficacy* as a sojourner. As you work through your transition period, you begin to develop a sense of self-efficacy as a sojourner and as a TCP. Self-efficacy in transition means that you realize you have become someone who can complete cross-culture transitions without losing your sense of personal identity along the way. Self-efficacy implies that you are accomplished in a specific area or that you are good at a specific skill or academic subject. It is quite different than self-esteem because a positive sense of self-efficacy develops over time in a specific area by working hard to succeed in that area. In contrast, self-esteem is the way you view yourself in general and is sometimes more dependent on outside influences than on your actual success in a given area. So, a rubric is just the tool that helps you see your success at transitioning – similar to when you follow a rubric to guide your progress in academic work. Each success allows you to build confidence and persistence as a successful cross-cultural sojourner and prepares you for your next transition journey. Finally, a person should use the Reacculturation Rubric to *Challenge the Fossils* in their life. Think of the fossils as those things that might be stumbling blocks for you as you leave your host culture or your current secure cultural environment and readjust in your new home, work, or school culture. The idea is that, just as a fossil is hard and rigid, some people get rather hard and inflexible when they meet difficulties in their transition journey. A fossilized Third Culture Person tends to stay in the same spot in their transition journey for too long and can develop negative attitudes toward people or perhaps make destructive life choices because they feel uncomfortable in their situation. Any person can fossilize in their transition journey no matter their age or the events in their transition experience. Even monocultural people can fossilize in their life journey if they do not continually work to make a successful transition at each different stage in their life.

My Personal Reacculturation Transition Story

About three years after moving from Thailand to Southern California, I recall thinking to myself, as I walked into my office building, *I feel normal again*! I had to stop and think through what *normal* meant to me and why the thought came to my mind at that particular time. First of all, *normal* meant that I didn't feel cold. I wasn't even wearing a jacket or carrying one just in case I would need it later in the day. Having lived in the tropics of South East Asia for 25 years, even Southern California felt cold most of the time except for the hottest two or three months of the year. So, to realize that I felt *normal*, temperature-wise, was a notable thought and an enjoyable moment. I was now hopeful that just maybe I had acclimatized to my current surroundings successfully. I also felt *normal* about my job. I realized that I was much less stressed because I had mastered new responsibilities and transitioned into the different work schedules that governed the hours in my day. I had also adapted to new community participation opportunities and belonged to several community groups. I have to admit that I was somewhat surprised that I had just then noticed feeling different about my current home culture and life situation. I was especially struck that it had taken three years to come to this realization. As a result, I realized that cross-culture transition takes both time and effort to fully complete. This realization has since inspired a sense of compassion for others who might be struggling through life transitions and has become the compelling reason for developing a guide for cross-culture transitions in the form of this Reacculturation Rubric.

A Transition Challenge for You

Here is a cross-culture transition challenge for you. After using the Reacculturation Rubric as a guide for reviewing your transition progress, you might identify an area where you are stuck or where you have *fossilized* in your transition process. Your next step is to challenge the "fossils" that seem to be hindering your progress. By challenging the fossils, I mean to attack the fossilized area head-on. Evaluate the area where you are fossilizing and purposely continue to reflect and determine your next steps. Work hard to succeed in each area of your reacculturation transition difficulty and remain flexible as you learn how to fit into your home (or new) culture. For example, if you are lonely, you must be willing to take action and work at developing healthy friendships rather than wait around and always expect others to reach out to you. A rubric is a tool that sheds light on where you are stuck in your reacculturation process. We call this step *challenging the barriers or fossils* that are blocking your successful transition. You don't want to become a fossilized TCP who is hardened by negative attitudes or stuck on being unhappy by constantly wishing for something you enjoyed in your host culture that is unavailable in your new culture. Again, a rubric is an effective tool for finding those areas of fossilization. A rubric also lets you know that others have gone before you and succeeded in their reacculturation transition journey. If you do find a place of fossilization, then seek help. The purpose of a rubric is to let you know things about your self-development as a sojourner so that you can take charge of your life and your Reacculturation Cross-culture Transition Process.

Reacculturation Cross-culture Transition Rubric

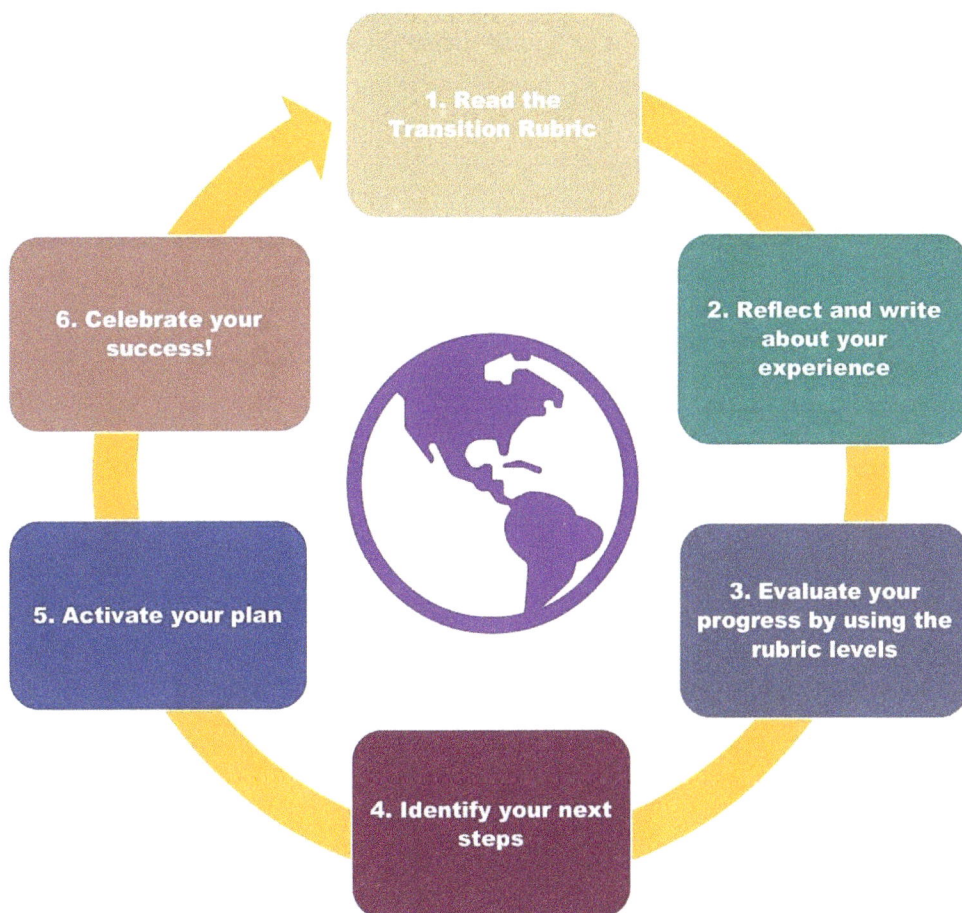

1. Read the Transition Rubric

2. Reflect and write about your experience

3. Evaluate your progress by using the rubric levels

4. Identify your next steps

5. Activate your plan

6. Celebrate your success!

Purposeful Reflection and Self-assessment by Using the Reacculturation Rubric

A rubric is used to provide direction and to assess progress at meeting the expectation or goal stated in the rubric. For example, teachers provide rubrics to guide students through an assignment so that learning occurs and students meet the standard of expected outcomes. Likewise, this Reacculturation Rubric can be used as a guide to help sojourners go healthily through their transition process. The following Reacculturation Rubric pages will help you reflect on and self-assess your progress and see exactly where you are and how you might be able to achieve a more satisfying transition to your next home or cultural environment. Each rubric page asks a few questions and provides space for answers as you consider each element in the rubric. I recommend you do this reflection work the first time you use the rubric and then a few months later and again in a year or so as you continue to grow through your Reacculturation Transition Process. Keep in mind that you could be reading this rubric before you leave your host culture or just a day after arriving in your transition culture… or it may be 20 years after you came back to your home culture. It really doesn't matter because this is a personal reflection activity that you can do on your own or in a family or group setting. Please take the time to complete each of the reflection activities. Be sure to note your progress, and do take time to *celebrate your success*.

Assessing Your Cross-culture Transition Journey Progress

Use the following six steps to guide your self-assessment journey. It is important to follow a systematic plan to guide you through your self-assessment journey so that you stay on track and complete each element of the rubric.

Step 1 – **Read** each element on the rubric and *assess* your current stage of transition by highlighting the words in the rubric that best describe your transition progress. Then record your score (1, 2, 3, or 4) in the score column and note specific details for each element on the assessment worksheet.

Step 2 – **Reflect** on and write about your experiences on the empty worksheet pages and add the date so that you can see your progress.

Step 3 – **Evaluate** your progress in each rubric area.

Step 4 – **Identify** your next steps of action to move forward in your transition process.

Step 5 – **Activate** your plan.

Step 6 – **Celebrate** your success each time you move forward on the rubric.

Reacculturation Cross-culture Transition Rubric

TCP Reacculturation Process Issues

	SCORE	LIMITED COMPETENCIES 1	DEVELOPING COMPETENCIES 2	PROFICIENT COMPETENCIES 3	ADVANCED COMPETENCIES 4
Reverse Culture Shock		➤ Experiences negative feelings toward home culture. ➤ Feels physically ill at times/often. ➤ Somewhat depressed. ➤ Feels trapped and can't understand why. ➤ Disappointed at changes in home culture. ➤ Longs for host culture experiences and relationships. ➤ Refuses comfort w/o host culture familiarities.	➤ Begins to accept changes in home culture. ➤ Can assuage homesick feelings by engaging in familiar (host culture) situations (e.g., food, phone calls to host country friends). ➤ Finds some comfort/pleasure in home culture activities and experiences.	➤ Rarely experiences excessive homesick feeling or longing for host culture but enjoys encountering host culture experiences in a healthy manner. ➤ Enjoys sharing host culture with friends and family. ➤ Feels satisfied/comfortable in both home and host cultures.	➤ No symptoms of reverse culture shock apparent. ➤ Fully functional in both cultures. ➤ Enjoys mutually fulfilling experiences in both cultures. ➤ Can create satisfying experiences in both home and host cultures (e.g., decorating home as in host/home culture, sharing artifacts or clothing in host/home culture).
Cultural Fatigue		➤ TCP experiences extreme fatigue at attempting to readjust in home culture. ➤ Must be hyper vigilant to interpret social cues and spoken message of home culture. ➤ Feels a need to escape and longs for familiarities of host culture. ➤ Sleep does not relieve fatigue.	➤ Notes areas of reacculturation difficulty and prepares accordingly. ➤ Plans ahead for new situations. ➤ Asks for help or advice when confronted with confusing situation. ➤ Recognizes need to pull back and regroup when fatigue is noticed. ➤ Looks for familiar (host culture) situations as a way to rest. ➤ Ready to attempt realignment with home culture.	➤ Makes multiple decisions daily involving appropriate cultural interactions. ➤ Has a sense of satisfaction concerning level of proficiency. ➤ Enjoys learning more about home culture. ➤ Notes changes that have occurred and plans to meet change in mature manner. ➤ Depends on new friends to help interpret social cues. ➤ Enjoys memories of host culture experiences but not fixated on them.	➤ Moves and interacts easily among peers w/o feeling fatigued or stressed. ➤ Has a developed sense of self-efficacy concerning interaction with peers and cultural events. ➤ Encounters new situations with confidence and enjoyment w/o experiencing unusual fatigue/stress. ➤ Maintains healthy attitude and memories of host culture. ➤ Enjoys both home and host cultures for different reasons.
Expectations of Home Culture		➤ Holds numerous unrealistic expectations of home culture. ➤ Cannot deal with changes in home culture. ➤ Holds friends and relatives captive in mind by unrealistic and impossible expectations.	➤ Begins to sort out unrealistic expectations from realistic expectations. ➤ Can verbalize areas of unrealistic expectations. ➤ Maintains negative or disappointed attitude in areas where expectations weren't met.	➤ Notes areas of realistic/unrealistic expectations. ➤ Does not hold negative attitude or disappointed attitude concerning unrealistic expectations (esp. if not met). ➤ Notes realistic expectations met.	➤ Able to discuss realistic and unrealistic expectations of home culture. ➤ Reacts appropriately in a variety of situations. ➤ Realizes/accepts/honors growth and change of friends/family during absence.
Stress/ Health Problems		➤ Often experiences reacculturation stress-related illness (e.g., stomach upset, heartburn, loss of sleep, itching, etc.). ➤ Panic attacks occur often/daily. ➤ Food allergies emerge or exacerbated. ➤ Doctors unable to pinpoint root cause of health problems.	➤ Experiences moderate stress-related physical effects. ➤ Able to tie events that caused stress to specific issues of readjustment.	➤ Able to complete daily responsibilities w/o stress or panic attacks. ➤ Realizes change is stressful and plans accordingly.	➤ Reacculturation stress does not hinder taking on responsibility. ➤ Enjoys taking on challenging/new types of responsibilities. ➤ Physical condition is within normal range.

11

TCP Marginalization Issues

	SCORE	LIMITED COMPETENCIES 1	DEVELOPING COMPETENCIES 2	PROFICIENT COMPETENCIES 3	ADVANCED COMPETENCIES 4
Loss of Place Church/Community		➤ Lacks sense of belonging in church or community organizations. ➤ Avoids contact w/community. States that they are not wanted or missed. ➤ Holds negative attitude toward all communities. ➤ Strong positive affinity toward (participation in) host communities in the area (e.g., church groups). ➤ Host community is viewed as perfect in all respects.	➤ Attends community functions. ➤ Willing to be a participant in community but not actively seeking participation. ➤ Tends to offer ideas from global perspective gained in host culture, but often over extends ideas and application of ideas. ➤ Has tendency to over commit, which leads to frustration.	➤ Honors/supports existing home culture community leadership. ➤ Willing to take lower position jobs and/or volunteers to take responsibilities even if at a lower level than held in host culture. ➤ Sees ways to suggest new ideas from global perspective w/o causing defensiveness in others.	➤ Actively involved in church and community. ➤ Feels a part of community. Maintains healthy relationship with host culture communities but is satisfied not to hold past role since s/he is not living in host country. ➤ Actively contributes ideas from positive global perspective w/o negative side effects. ➤ Developed social capital in all areas.
Professional Loss		➤ Has no job or no capacity to actively seek employment. ➤ Feels alienated from colleagues in field. ➤ Is de-skilled in discipline/technology. ➤ Depressed, bitter, angry, or resentful attitude. ➤ Blames self, employer, host culture. ➤ Feels like s/he has given of self w/no return on personal investment.	➤ Feels de-skilled but is now willing to learn new skills. ➤ Takes classes/training to regain professional losses. ➤ Asks for help from employer/sending organization. ➤ Avidly seeks employment. ➤ Takes pride in work even if not in area of past employment.	➤ Takes any available job with notion that one can regain skills and retrain for new job. ➤ Willing to take lower position and is thankful for any new opportunity. ➤ Does not expect to be able to apply TCP experience immediately. ➤ Honors/values new boss and co-workers even though less experienced than the TCP in many areas.	➤ Has regained lost skills and experience. ➤ Feels like s/he is operating at full competence in field/area. ➤ Is able to utilize TCP experience in appropriate measure/manner. ➤ Feels a sense of affirmation or confirmation in new role. ➤ Willing to stay put even if s/he is used to moving often.
Loss of Language		➤ Feels robbed of something special w/o a place to use the host language. ➤ Attempts to use language in inappropriate manner/places. ➤ Feels depressed because s/he cannot communicate to fullest extent. ➤ Makes no effort to change attitude and regain skills in home culture language. ➤ Feels happy or secure when calling host culture friends and sometimes speaks in negative terms concerning home culture in host culture language.	➤ Thinks in host language at times and uses it when appropriate. ➤ Seeks opportunities to use host language. Keeps practicing so as not to forget host language. ➤ Willing to speak home language more extensively.	➤ Proficient in both home/host languages. ➤ Positive understanding of when to use or not use host language. ➤ Feels sense of complete communication ability in home language. ➤ Still enjoys reading/writing/speaking in host language but not disabled without using it.	➤ Has balanced bi-lingual language skills and appropriate sense of when to use each language. ➤ Shares host language when appropriate. Finds effective and meaningful ways to use host language. ➤ Has a sense of completeness when there is use for both languages. ➤ Has a secure sense of self w/o using host language.

TCP Support and Belonging Issues

	LIMITED COMPETENCIES 1	DEVELOPING COMPETENCIES 2	PROFICIENT COMPETENCIES 3	ADVANCED COMPETENCIES 4	SCORE
Family	‣ Feels estranged from immediate family members. ‣ Takes offense at most of what they do or say. ‣ Feels hurt that they are not fully devoted to sharing TCP's experiences. ‣ Feels frustrated at not being able to fully share in family experiences that have happened during the TCP's sojourn. ‣ Resents time apart. ‣ Seems unable to close gap on feelings of distance in relationships.	‣ Willing to work at becoming part of the family on home culture terms and turf. ‣ Listens more than talks. ‣ Values family members for their life experiences just as much as s/he wishes to be valued for host culture experiences.	‣ Shares on a give/take basis with family events, work, and experiences. ‣ Values family relationships more than sharing TCP experiences. ‣ Willing to take a passive role and learn new things about family members. ‣ Appreciates family members and the family roles.	‣ Has shared TCP experiences sufficiently to feel respect and awe of family members. ‣ Feels fully supported in reacculturation process. ‣ Realizes family is important and willing to do what it takes to regain losses due to absence as a TCP. ‣ Finds family relationships rewarding and helpful/supportive to all family members.	
Friends	‣ Dominates conversations. ‣ Expects friends to be exactly the same as before leaving. ‣ Angry at anything that has changed during time away. ‣ Clings to or values TCP experience more than home culture friends. ‣ Leaves friends and believes they are not worth the time and effort of rebuilding friendships. ‣ Finds excuses not to socialize due to time and emotional effort of rebuilding friendships.	‣ Willing to listen and put in time and effort to rebuild friendships. ‣ Takes a few risks and invites friends to engage in host culture experiences as a means to build a bridge between home and host cultures.	‣ Realizes that healthy changes must occur throughout friendships. ‣ Allows friends to support TCP even if the type of support is different than experienced while in host culture.	‣ Has a good mixture of friends from both home and host cultures. ‣ Feels validated and is able to validate friends from both cultures. ‣ Finds that time does not change friendships from either culture, and when chances to be together occur it is as if no time has passed. ‣ The conversation picks up where left off, and bridges between lives have been rebuilt.	
Groups	‣ Avoids church, community, or groups of friends. ‣ Finds little/no support from groups. ‣ Finds groups intimidating and threatening. ‣ Relies strongly on group support from host culture. ‣ Relies on stature gained from group memberships in host culture for sense of self.	‣ Begins to join groups to find support and a sense of identity. ‣ Becomes discouraged with group activities easily and feels taken advantage of if asked to participate. ‣ Wants recognition but does not want to earn the right to be respected or recognized. ‣ Believes the group lacks a global vision or that the group is not interested in finding a remedy for the world's problems, etc. ‣ Prefers/actively pursues the big fish in little pond feeling when being in control of a group through leadership roles.	‣ Belongs to one or a few groups that help define values and share personal interests. ‣ Utilizes TCP experience to support meaningful group participation. ‣ Is willing to participate in a number of different types of roles within group structure. ‣ Can be satisfied with much recognition or no recognition.	‣ Has bonded with church and community groups that share like values. ‣ Is involved with charitable groups, civic groups, and other groups that offer service to community. ‣ Is OK with being the small fish in a big pond. ‣ Willing to contribute even if not in charge of the group. ‣ Finds comradery and support and feeling of significance through meaningful group memberships. ‣ Can contribute in leadership positions successfully.	

13

	Limited Competencies 1	Developing Competencies 2	Proficient Competencies 3	Advanced Competencies 4
SCORE				
TCP Cultural Heritage Issues				
Cultural Uniqueness	➤ Highly overvalues/undervalues TCP experience. ➤ Believes TCP experience is the only worthwhile experience. ➤ Devalues home culture as having nothing unique.	➤ Values the TCP experience more than the monoculture experience but does not allow view to limit progress in the reacculturation process. ➤ Beginning to see some value in home culture.	➤ Is beginning to see value to cultural heritage in a balanced view. ➤ Seems to realize positive/negative sides to the TCP experience. ➤ Current view allows the TCP to move ahead in the reacculturation process with awe and eagerness for life's next events/stages.	➤ A balanced view of TCP experience that appreciates and values the TCP experience. ➤ Realizes that both host and home cultures provide worthwhile and unique experiences that enhance one's life. ➤ Uses heritage as a stabilizing tool as part of one's identity and without a limiting effect.
Personal Meaning and Positive Cultural Elements	➤ Inappropriate/lack of development of personal meaning from the TCP experience. ➤ Seems distant and uncommunicative regarding TCP experience. ➤ Detached, in own world, surface thinker concerning TCP experience. ➤ Finds few/no positive elements to the TCP experience. ➤ Feels bitter toward sending agency or parents for imposing the TCP life on subject.	➤ Is somewhat reflective concerning the personal meaning of TCP experience but does not value the experience as a life enhancement. ➤ Sees some positive elements to the TCP experience. ➤ Realizes being different is OK and may even be a positive aspect of cultural heritage.	➤ Is reflective concerning TCP experience. ➤ Personal meaning concerning TCP experience is emerging in an appropriate measure. ➤ Finds positive elements in personal development from TCP experience. ➤ Enjoys being different or changed as a result of the TCP experience. ➤ Has a balanced view of positive/negative changes in TCP cultural elements.	➤ Has developed deep and personal meaning from the TCP experience. ➤ Allows the TCP experience to enhance meaningfulness of life in a positive manner. ➤ Shares meaningful TCP stories with family and friends. ➤ Realizes that there are pros and cons to the TCP experience. ➤ Enjoys the positive aspects and allows those to enhance sense of self. ➤ Takes charge of the negative aspects and learns from the experiences and allows them to inform his/her future.
Rootedness	➤ Lacks sense of rootedness in home culture. ➤ Exaggerates roots or ties to host culture. ➤ Unrealistic attitude toward what it means to be rooted. ➤ Takes off every few months or couple of years to find him/herself. ➤ Vagabond type of lifestyle. ➤ Allows lack of rootedness to destroy relationships with family and work. ➤ Fakes rootedness when experiencing social pressure.	➤ Exercises moderate control of desire to flee the scene. ➤ Realizes the importance of keeping a balance between both home and host cultures. ➤ Experiences strong desires to travel or return to host culture but maintains job and relationships. ➤ Discusses travel with spouse, friends, or family appropriately. ➤ Evaluates current situation with a fairly balanced view.	➤ Has a sense of roots based in solid worldview. ➤ Holds higher values that do not change with new or old cultural experiences. ➤ Allows TCP roots to provide foundation in both home and host cultures. ➤ Shares roots in an appropriate measure with family and friends. ➤ Roots provide source and stability to engage in activities of generativity.	➤ Firmly rooted in values and clearly-held beliefs irrespective of home or host culture. ➤ Rooted in unique cultural heritage that has emerged between both home and host cultures. ➤ Feels at home where located. ➤ Values relationships over roots and finds ways to connect or reconnect with roots of heritage from both cultures. ➤ Highly involved in different types of generativity activities.

TCP Re-entry Preparation Issues

	LIMITED COMPETENCIES 1	DEVELOPING COMPETENCIES 2	PROFICIENT COMPETENCIES 3	ADVANCED COMPETENCIES 4	SCORE
Social Preparation	➤ Socially unprepared for re-entry. ➤ Seems shocked at the changes in home culture and social expectations of peers. ➤ Finds negative factors with all social encounters. ➤ Generally finds fault with home culture and imagines a perfect world in host culture. ➤ Feels betrayed as a result of the hype presented in host culture and finds s/he is no longer the big fish in a small pond…rather a fish out of water! ➤ Unwilling to give up distinctively host culture social actions that have a *putting off* effect on peers.	➤ Willing to give socialization a try. ➤ Takes time to think about social events and plan for successful encounters. ➤ Extends invitations to a few acquaintances with caution. ➤ Is willing to persist with social efforts knowing it takes time to make new friends.	➤ Has a positive attitude toward making new friends. ➤ Is willing to work hard and not give up during reacculturation process. ➤ Develops new social capital while drawing on TCP pool of social capital in transition period. ➤ Realizes social capital may be in different pools than host culture peers.	➤ Is socially adept in both cultures. ➤ Took advantage of transition workshops prior to leaving host culture. ➤ Has a positive sense of self-efficacy in areas of social development. ➤ Can go with the flow when interacting socially. ➤ Maintains boundaries and moral values regardless of peer pressure.	
Academic Preparation	➤ Believes that TCP academic preparation exceeds that of peers. ➤ Either is ill-prepared or differently prepared for academic rigors. ➤ Unable to incorporate TCP experience in a supporting manner. ➤ Has strong opinions (either positive or negative) about host culture people and their academic preparation.	➤ Looks for and receives help in learning the ropes of schooling in home culture. ➤ Begins to accept a realistic view of academic preparation. ➤ Notes areas of expertise and areas of deficiency in academic preparation. ➤ Can interact with peers on academic matters w/o a sense of superiority or inferiority.	➤ Begins to realize s/he needs to study hard in order to advance in home culture educational situations. ➤ Realizes the need to go back to school for retraining. ➤ Appreciates educational opportunities offered in home culture. ➤ Accepts responsibility for gaps in learning and willing to put in the effort to gain competence in weak areas.	➤ Has advanced academic preparation. ➤ Can assimilate academic preparation and TCP experience into current educational experience. ➤ Makes conscience effort to learn new things from home culture school even if students are generally less advanced. ➤ Is humble in attitude and willing to make mistakes. ➤ Realizes there are highly intelligent students in both cultures.	
Professional Preparation	➤ De-skilled and unprepared for re-entry into profession. ➤ Unable to admit that there are areas where TCP has become de-skilled. ➤ Unwilling to retrain or take pre/post-entry preparation courses offered through sending agency. ➤ Realizes s/he is lacking in areas but fearful of changes. ➤ Feels overwhelmed with all the changes of returning to home culture so cannot begin retraining.	➤ Realizes the need for retraining. ➤ Looking for opportunities for retraining. ➤ Takes short courses or seminar type training. ➤ Looks for new areas to expand in professionally.	➤ Is enjoying new opportunities for professional growth. ➤ Finds collegial support in training or educational opportunities. ➤ Is creative in looking at situations "outside of the box." ➤ Refuses to feel discouraged as a result of missed opportunities in home culture.	➤ Uses TCP experience as professional capital to inform new opportunities. ➤ Willing to take any job while at the same time retraining and preparing for new professional opportunities. ➤ Maintains positive attitude even though s/he may have experienced being passed over for promotions.	

General Overview of Timeline for Reacculturation

1 Year	2 Years	3 Years	3+ Years
➤ Beginning stages of reacculturation. ➤ A good time to stop and take stock of progress in each area. ➤ Evaluate progress and decide which areas should receive more attention. ➤ Realize reacculturation is a lengthy process and it takes time and effort.	➤ Review personal progress of reacculturation process and notice development since the one-year mark. ➤ Take specific steps to shore up areas of difficulty. ➤ Ask accountability partners to help keep reacculturation process on track. ➤ Note vulnerable areas where TCP feels like s/he is threatened and address each area with realistic goals. ➤ Note any areas of "fossilization" and begin to challenge them.	➤ Three years seems to be a stabilizing point in the readjustment process. ➤ TCPs have had opportunity to learn the ropes of a new job, regain family relationships, resettle in the community, and resume cultural competency. ➤ TCPs have had opportunity to invest social capital wisely. ➤ TCPs are generally beginning to feel stabilized in relationships as well as in productivity. ➤ A sense of self-efficacy concerning reacculturation competencies has developed or is developing in most areas. ➤ Has noted and challenged areas of fossilization.	➤ For some TCPs it may take longer than three years to accomplish full reacculturation competencies. ➤ Reacculturation goals may not be complete in any one of the areas mentioned but a lag noticed in an area should now be met with a purposeful goal. ➤ It would be wise to seek a counselor to prioritize efforts in lagging area(s) in order not to stagnate/fossilize. ➤ Keep in mind that change and growth are healthy if managed wisely. ➤ All people experience life-long change/growth. ➤ A prepared mind is able to take positive advantage of growth opportunities throughout life.

Meaning of Scoring Results

1-point scores/ Overall score of 16–27	2-point scores/ Overall score of 28–39	3-point scores/ Overall score of 40–51	4-point scores/ Overall score of 52–64
➤ Might indicate a degree of fossilization in a specific area or areas. ➤ Fossilization implies that the reacculturation process has stopped at a specific point in a given area. ➤ TCP needs help in specific areas (e.g., language development, job training, relationship building) in order to move forward. ➤ Needs a mentor/accountability group.	➤ The TCP is moving forward in attempting to become adept at functioning in home culture after TCP experience. ➤ Fossilization is probable if positive progress does not continue. ➤ TCP stagnates in an area. ➤ This is a normal stage to pass through…but the key is to pass through the stage and to not remain in the stage.	➤ Suggests that adequacy has been reached in a specific area or areas. ➤ It is possible to reach a developmentally adequate range in one area and lag behind in another area. ➤ There is still room for growth in the reacculturation process. ➤ The TCP is able to identify areas of strengths and weaknesses.	➤ At this stage of development, the TCP experience serves as an important completion of a positive sense-of-self. ➤ Aspects of the TCP experience serve to enhance the TCP's life w/o controlling his/her life. ➤ The TCP is successful at pinpointing strengths and weaknesses and adjusts accordingly.

16

Reacculturation Cross-culture Transition Rubric and Assessment Worksheets

1. Read the Transition Rubric

2. Reflect and write about your experience

3. Evaluate your progress by using the rubric levels

4. Identify your next steps

5. Activate your plan

6. Celebrate your success!

Reacculturation Cross-culture Transition Rubric Assessment Worksheets

TCP Reacculturation Process Issues

SCORE	LIMITED COMPETENCIES 1	DEVELOPING COMPETENCIES 2	PROFICIENT COMPETENCIES 3	ADVANCED COMPETENCIES 4
Reverse Culture Shock	➢ Experiences negative feelings toward home culture. ➢ Feels physically ill at times/often. ➢ Somewhat depressed. ➢ Feels trapped and can't understand why. ➢ Disappointed at changes in home culture. ➢ Longs for host culture experiences and relationships. ➢ Refuses comfort w/o host culture familiarities.	➢ Begins to accept changes in home culture. ➢ Can assuage homesick feelings by engaging in familiar (host culture) situations (e.g., food, phone calls to host country friends). ➢ Finds some comfort/pleasure in home culture activities and experiences.	➢ Rarely experiences excessive homesick feeling or longing for host culture but enjoys encountering host culture experiences in a healthy manner. ➢ Enjoys sharing host culture with friends and family. ➢ Feels satisfied/comfortable in both home and host cultures.	➢ No symptoms of reverse culture shock apparent. ➢ Fully functional in both cultures. ➢ Enjoys mutually fulfilling experiences in both cultures. ➢ Can create satisfying experiences in both home and host cultures (e.g., decorating home as in host/home culture, sharing artifacts or clothing in host/home culture).
Cultural Fatigue	➢ TCP experiences extreme fatigue at attempting to readjust in home culture. ➢ Must be hyper vigilant to interpret social cues and spoken message of home culture. ➢ Feels a need to escape and longs for familiarities of host culture. ➢ Sleep does not relieve fatigue.	➢ Notes areas of reacculturation difficulty and prepares accordingly. ➢ Plans ahead for new situations. ➢ Asks for help or advice when confronted with confusing situation. ➢ Recognizes need to pull back and regroup when fatigue is noticed. ➢ Looks for familiar (host culture) situations as a way to rest. ➢ Ready to attempt realignment with home culture.	➢ Makes multiple decisions daily involving appropriate cultural interactions. ➢ Has a sense of satisfaction concerning level of proficiency. ➢ Enjoys learning more about home culture. ➢ Notes changes that have occurred and plans to meet change in mature manner. ➢ Depends on new friends to help interpret social cues. ➢ Enjoys memories of host culture experiences but not fixated on them.	➢ Moves and interacts easily among peers w/o feeling fatigued or stressed. ➢ Has a developed sense of self-efficacy concerning interaction with peers and cultural events. ➢ Encounters new situations with confidence and enjoyment w/o experiencing unusual fatigue/stress. ➢ Maintains healthy attitude and memories of host culture. ➢ Enjoys both home and host cultures for different reasons.
Expectations of Home Culture	➢ Holds numerous unrealistic expectations of home culture. ➢ Cannot deal with changes in home culture. ➢ Holds friends and relatives captive in mind by unrealistic and impossible expectations.	➢ Begins to sort out unrealistic expectations from realistic expectations. ➢ Can verbalize areas of unrealistic expectations. ➢ Maintains negative or disappointed attitude in areas where expectations weren't met.	➢ Notes areas of realistic/unrealistic expectations. ➢ Does not hold negative attitude or disappointed attitude concerning unrealistic expectations (esp. if not met). ➢ Notes realistic expectations met.	➢ Able to discuss realistic and unrealistic expectations of home culture. ➢ Reacts appropriately in a variety of situations. ➢ Realizes/accepts/honors growth and change of friends/family during absence.
Stress/ Health Problems	➢ Often experiences reacculturation stress-related illness (e.g., stomach upset, heartburn, loss of sleep, itching, etc.). ➢ Panic attacks occur often/daily. ➢ Food allergies emerge or exacerbated. ➢ Doctors unable to pinpoint root cause of health problems.	➢ Experiences moderate stress-related physical effects. ➢ Able to tie events that caused stress to specific issues of readjustment.	➢ Able to complete daily responsibilities w/o stress or panic attacks. ➢ Realizes change is stressful and plans accordingly.	➢ Reacculturation stress does not hinder taking on responsibility. ➢ Enjoys taking on challenging/new types of responsibilities. ➢ Physical condition is within normal range.

TCP Reacculturation Process Issues Assessment

	LIMITED COMPETENCIES 1	DEVELOPING COMPETENCIES 2	PROFICIENT COMPETENCIES 3	ADVANCED COMPETENCIES 4	SCORE
Reverse Culture Shock	Record your experiences here:	Record your experiences here and celebrate your growth and development:	Record your experiences here and celebrate your proficient success:	Record your experiences here and celebrate your advanced successes:	
Cultural Fatigue					
Expectations of Home Culture					
Stress/ Health Problems					

20

TCP Reacculturation Process Issues Reflection

Identify Where You Are on the Rubric	Highlight the phrases/descriptors that best describe your current experience in the rubric. Which column do the majority of your highlighted phrases fall into? This suggests where you are on the Reacculturation continuum.
Write About Your Experiences	Write about a recent experience you've had that reflects a Reacculturation Process problem in some area of your life.
Apply Your Knowledge	Apply: What strengths do you bring from your background? What weaknesses do you need to be aware of?
Next Steps	What are your **next steps** to address the stressors or liabilities you are currently experiencing? List below:

TCP Marginalization Issues

	LIMITED COMPETENCIES 1	DEVELOPING COMPETENCIES 2	PROFICIENT COMPETENCIES 3	ADVANCED COMPETENCIES 4
Loss of Place Church/Community	➢ Lacks sense of belonging in church or community organizations. ➢ Avoids contact w/community. States that they are not wanted or missed. ➢ Holds negative attitude toward all communities. ➢ Strong positive affinity toward (participation in) host communities in the area (e.g., church groups). ➢ Host community is viewed as perfect in all respects.	➢ Attends community functions. ➢ Willing to be a participant in community but not actively seeking participation. ➢ Tends to offer ideas from global perspective gained in host culture, but often over extends ideas and application of ideas. ➢ Has tendency to over commit, which leads to frustration.	➢ Honors/supports existing home culture community leadership. ➢ Willing to take lower position jobs and/or volunteers to take responsibilities even if at a lower level than held in host culture. ➢ Sees ways to suggest new ideas from global perspective w/o causing defensiveness in others.	➢ Actively involved in church and community. ➢ Feels a part of community. Maintains healthy relationship with host culture communities but is satisfied not to hold past role since s/he is not living in host country. ➢ Actively contributes ideas from positive global perspective w/o negative side effects. ➢ Developed social capital in all areas.
Professional Loss	➢ Has no job or no capacity to actively seek employment. ➢ Feels alienated from colleagues in field. ➢ Is de-skilled in discipline/technology. ➢ Depressed, bitter, angry, or resentful attitude. ➢ Blames self, employer, host culture. ➢ Feels like s/he has given of self w/no return on personal investment.	➢ Feels de-skilled but is now willing to learn new skills. ➢ Takes classes/training to regain professional losses. ➢ Asks for help from employer/sending organization. ➢ Avidly seeks employment. ➢ Takes pride in work even if not in area of past employment.	➢ Takes any available job with notion that one can regain skills and retrain for new job. ➢ Willing to take lower position and is thankful for any new opportunity. ➢ Does not expect to be able to apply TCP experience immediately. ➢ Honors/values new boss and co-workers even though less experienced than the TCP in many areas.	➢ Has regained lost skills and experience. ➢ Feels like s/he is operating at full competence in field/area. ➢ Is able to utilize TCP experience in appropriate measure/manner. ➢ Feels a sense of affirmation or confirmation in new role. ➢ Willing to stay put even if s/he is used to moving often.
Loss of Language	➢ Feels robbed of something special w/o a place to use the host language. ➢ Attempts to use language in inappropriate manner/places. ➢ Feels depressed because s/he cannot communicate to fullest extent. ➢ Makes no effort to change attitude and regain skills in home culture language. ➢ Feels happy or secure when calling host culture friends and sometimes speaks in negative terms concerning home culture in host culture language.	➢ Thinks in host language at times and uses it when appropriate. ➢ Seeks opportunities to use host language. Keeps practicing so as not to forget host language. ➢ Willing to speak home language more extensively.	➢ Proficient in both home/host languages. ➢ Positive understanding of when to use or not use host language. ➢ Feels sense of complete communication ability in home language. ➢ Still enjoys reading/writing/speaking in host language but not disabled without using it.	➢ Has balanced bi-lingual language skills and appropriate sense of when to use each language. ➢ Shares host language when appropriate. ➢ Finds effective and meaningful ways to use host language. ➢ Has a sense of completeness when there is use for both languages. ➢ Has a secure sense of self w/o using host language.

SCORE

TCP Marginalization Issues Assessment

	LIMITED COMPETENCIES 1	DEVELOPING COMPETENCIES 2	PROFICIENT COMPETENCIES 3	ADVANCED COMPETENCIES 4	SCORE
Loss of Place Church/Community	Record your experiences here:	Record your experiences here and celebrate your growth and development	Record your experiences here and celebrate your proficient success:	Record your experiences here and celebrate your advanced successes	
Professional Loss					
Loss of Language					

23

TCP Marginalization Issues Reflections

Highlight the phrases/descriptors that best describe your current experience in the rubric. Which column do the majority of your highlighted phrases fall into? This suggests where you are on the Marginalization Issues continuum.

Write about a recent experience you've had that reflects being marginalized in some area of your life.

Apply: What strengths do you bring from your background to overcome being marginalized? What weaknesses do you need to be aware of?

What are your **next steps** to address the stressors or liabilities you are currently experiencing? List below:

24

SCORE	LIMITED COMPETENCIES 1	DEVELOPING COMPETENCIES 2	PROFICIENT COMPETENCIES 3	ADVANCED COMPETENCIES 4
TCP Support and Belonging Issues				
Family	➢ Feels estranged from immediate family members. ➢ Takes offense at most of what they do or say. ➢ Feels hurt that they are not fully devoted to sharing TCP's experiences. ➢ Feels frustrated at not being able to fully share in family experiences that have happened during the TCP's sojourn. ➢ Resents time apart. ➢ Seems unable to close gap on feelings of distance in relationships.	➢ Willing to work at becoming part of the family on home culture terms and turf. ➢ Listens more than talks. ➢ Values family members for their life experiences just as much as s/he wishes to be valued for host culture experiences.	➢ Shares on a give/take basis with family events, work, and experiences. ➢ Values family relationships more than sharing TCP experiences. ➢ Willing to take a passive role and learn new things about family members. ➢ Appreciates family members and the family roles.	➢ Has shared TCP experiences sufficiently to feel respect and awe of family members. ➢ Feels fully supported in reacculturation process. ➢ Realizes family is important and willing to do what it takes to regain losses due to absence as a TCP. ➢ Finds family relationships rewarding and helpful/supportive to all family members.
Friends	➢ Dominates conversations. ➢ Expects friends to be exactly the same as before leaving. ➢ Angry at anything that has changed during time away. ➢ Clings to or values TCP experience more than home culture friends. ➢ Leaves friends and believes they are not worth the time and effort of rebuilding friendships. ➢ Finds excuses not to socialize due to time and emotional effort of rebuilding friendships.	➢ Willing to listen and put in time and effort to rebuild friendships. ➢ Takes a few risks and invites friends to engage in host culture experiences as a means to build a bridge between home and host cultures.	➢ Realizes that healthy changes must occur throughout friendships. ➢ Allows friends to support TCP even if the type of support is different than experienced while in host culture.	➢ Has a good mixture of friends from both home and host cultures. ➢ Feels validated and is able to validate friends from both cultures. ➢ Finds that time does not change friendships from either culture, and when chances to be together occur it is as if no time has passed. ➢ The conversation picks up where left off, and bridges between lives have been rebuilt.
Groups	➢ Avoids church, community, or groups of friends. ➢ Finds little/no support from groups. ➢ Finds groups intimidating and threatening. ➢ Relies strongly on group support from host culture. ➢ Relies on stature gained from group memberships in host culture for sense of self.	➢ Begins to join groups to find support and a sense of identity. ➢ Becomes discouraged with group activities easily and feels taken advantage of if asked to participate. ➢ Wants recognition but does not want to earn the right to be respected or recognized. ➢ Believes the group lacks a global vision or that the group is not interested in finding a remedy for the world's problems, etc. ➢ Prefers/actively pursues the big fish in little pond feeling when being in control of a group through leadership roles.	➢ Belongs to one or a few groups that help define values and share personal interests. ➢ Utilizes TCP experience to support meaningful group participation. ➢ Is willing to participate in a number of different types of roles within group structure. ➢ Can be satisfied with much recognition or no recognition.	➢ Has bonded with church and community groups that share like values. ➢ Is involved with charitable groups, civic groups, and other groups that offer service to community. ➢ Is OK with being the small fish in a big pond. ➢ Willing to contribute even if not in charge of the group. ➢ Finds comradery and support and feeling of significance through meaningful group memberships. ➢ Can contribute in leadership positions successfully.

TCP Support and Belonging Issues Assessment

	LIMITED COMPETENCIES 1	DEVELOPING COMPETENCIES 2	PROFICIENT COMPETENCIES 3	ADVANCED COMPETENCIES 4	SCORE
Family	Record your experiences here:	Record your experiences here and celebrate your growth and development:	Record your experiences here and celebrate your proficient success:	Record your experiences here and celebrate your advanced successes:	
Friends					
Groups					

26

TCP Support and Belonging Issues Reflection

Identify Where You Are on the Rubric	Highlight the phrases/descriptors that best describe your current experience in the rubric. Which column do the majority of your highlighted phrases fall into? This suggests where you are on the Support and Belonging Reacculturation Issues continuum.
Write About Your Experiences	Write about a recent experience you've had that reflects a lack of Support or Belonging in some area of your life.
Apply Your Knowledge	Apply: What strengths do you bring from your background? What weaknesses do you need to be aware of?
Next Steps	What are your **next steps** to address the stressors or liabilities you are currently experiencing? List below:

	LIMITED COMPETENCIES 1	DEVELOPING COMPETENCIES 2	PROFICIENT COMPETENCIES 3	ADVANCED COMPETENCIES 4	SCORE
TCP Cultural Heritage Issues					
Cultural Uniqueness	➤ Highly overvalues/undervalues TCP experience. ➤ Believes TCP experience is the only worthwhile experience. ➤ Devalues home culture as having nothing unique.	➤ Values the TCP experience more than the monoculture experience but does not allow view to limit progress in the reacculturation process. ➤ Beginning to see some value in home culture.	➤ Is beginning to see value to cultural heritage in a balanced view. ➤ Seems to realize positive/negative sides to the TCP experience. ➤ Current view allows the TCP to move ahead in the reacculturation process with awe and eagerness for life's next events/stages.	➤ A balanced view of TCP experience that appreciates and values the TCP experience. ➤ Realizes that both host and home cultures provide worthwhile and unique experiences that enhance one's life. ➤ Uses heritage as a stabilizing tool as part of one's identity and without a limiting effect.	
Personal Meaning and Positive Cultural Elements	➤ Inappropriate/lack of development of personal meaning from the TCP experience. ➤ Seems distant and uncommunicative regarding TCP experience. ➤ Detached, in own world, surface thinker concerning TCP experience. ➤ Finds few/no positive elements to the TCP experience. ➤ Feels bitter toward sending agency or parents for imposing the TCP life on subject.	➤ Is somewhat reflective concerning the personal meaning of TCP experience but does not value the experience as a life enhancement. ➤ Sees some positive elements to the TCP experience. ➤ Realizes being different is OK and may even be a positive aspect of cultural heritage.	➤ Is reflective concerning TCP experience. ➤ Personal meaning concerning TCP experience is emerging in an appropriate measure. ➤ Finds positive elements in personal development from TCP experience. ➤ Enjoys being different or changed as a result of the TCP experience. ➤ Has a balanced view of positive/negative changes in TCP cultural elements.	➤ Has developed deep and personal meaning from the TCP experience. ➤ Allows the TCP experience to enhance meaningfulness of life in a positive manner. ➤ Shares meaningful TCP stories with family and friends. ➤ Realizes that there are pros and cons to the TCP experience. ➤ Enjoys the positive aspects and allows those to enhance sense of self. ➤ Takes charge of the negative aspects and learns from the experiences and allows them to inform his/her future.	
Rootedness	➤ Lacks sense of rootedness in home culture. ➤ Exaggerates roots or ties to host culture. ➤ Unrealistic attitude toward what it means to be rooted. ➤ Takes off every few months or couple of years to find him/herself. ➤ Vagabond type of lifestyle. ➤ Allows lack of rootedness to destroy relationships with family and work. ➤ Fakes rootedness when experiencing social pressure.	➤ Exercises moderate control of desire to flee the scene. ➤ Realizes the importance of keeping a balance between both home and host cultures. ➤ Experiences strong desires to travel or return to host culture but maintains job and relationships. ➤ Discusses travel with spouse, friends, or family appropriately. ➤ Evaluates current situation with a fairly balanced view.	➤ Has a sense of roots based in solid worldview. ➤ Holds higher values that do not change with new or old cultural experiences. ➤ Allows TCP roots to provide foundation in both home and host cultures. ➤ Shares roots in an appropriate measure with family and friends. ➤ Roots provide source and stability to engage in activities of generativity.	➤ Firmly rooted in values and dearly-held beliefs irrespective of home or host culture. ➤ Rooted in unique cultural heritage that has emerged between both home and host cultures. ➤ Feels at home where located. ➤ Values relationships over roots and finds ways to connect or reconnect with roots of heritage from both cultures. ➤ Highly involved in different types of generativity activities.	

TCP Cultural Heritage Assessment

	LIMITED COMPETENCIES 1	DEVELOPING COMPETENCIES 2	PROFICIENT COMPETENCIES 3	ADVANCED COMPETENCIES 4	SCORE
Cultural Uniqueness	Record your experiences here:	Record your experiences here and celebrate your growth and development:	Record your experiences here and celebrate your proficient success:	Record your experiences here and celebrate your advanced successes:	
Personal Meaning and Positive Cultural Elements					
Rootedness					

29

TCP Cultural Heritage Reflection

Identify Where You Are on the Rubric	Highlight the phrases/descriptors that best describe your current experience in the rubric. Which column do the majority of your highlighted phrases fall into? This suggests where you are on the Cultural Heritage Reacculturation Issues continuum.
Write About Your Experiences	Write about a recent experience you've had that reflects being stuck in your Cultural Heritage in some area of your life.
Apply Your Knowledge	Apply: What strengths do you bring from your background? What weaknesses do you need to be aware of?
Next Steps	What are your **next steps** to address the stressors or liabilities you are currently experiencing? List below:

30

	LIMITED COMPETENCIES 1	DEVELOPING COMPETENCIES 2	PROFICIENT COMPETENCIES 3	ADVANCED COMPETENCIES 4	SCORE
TCP Re-entry Preparation Issues					
Social Preparation	➤ Socially unprepared for re-entry. ➤ Seems shocked at the changes in home culture and social expectations of peers. ➤ Finds negative factors with all social encounters. ➤ Generally finds fault with home culture and imagines a perfect world in host culture. ➤ Feels betrayed as a result of the hype presented in host culture and finds s/he is no longer the big fish in a small pond...rather a fish out of water! ➤ Unwilling to give up distinctively host culture social actions that have a *putting off* effect on peers.	➤ Willing to give socialization a try. ➤ Takes time to think about social events and plan for successful encounters. ➤ Extends invitations to a few acquaintances with caution. ➤ Is willing to persist with social efforts knowing it takes time to make new friends.	➤ Has a positive attitude toward making new friends. ➤ Is willing to work hard and not give up during reacculturation process. ➤ Develops new social capital while drawing on TCP pool of social capital in transition period. ➤ Realizes social capital may be in different pools than host culture peers.	➤ Is socially adept in both cultures. ➤ Took advantage of transition workshops prior to leaving host culture. ➤ Has a positive sense of self-efficacy in areas of social development. ➤ Can go with the flow when interacting socially. ➤ Maintains boundaries and moral values regardless of peer pressure.	
Academic Preparation	➤ Believes that TCP academic preparation exceeds that of peers. ➤ Either is ill-prepared or differently prepared for academic rigors. ➤ Unable to incorporate TCP experience in a supporting manner. ➤ Has strong opinions (either positive or negative) about host culture people and their academic preparation.	➤ Looks for and receives help in learning the ropes of schooling in home culture. ➤ Begins to accept a realistic view of academic preparation. ➤ Notes areas of expertise and areas of deficiency in academic preparation. ➤ Can interact with peers on academic matters w/o a sense of superiority or inferiority.	➤ Begins to realize s/he needs to study hard in order to advance in home culture educational situations. ➤ Realizes the need to go back to school for retraining. ➤ Appreciates educational opportunities offered in home culture. ➤ Accepts responsibility for gaps in learning and willing to put in the effort to gain competence in weak areas.	➤ Has advanced academic preparation. ➤ Can assimilate academic preparation and TCP experience into current educational experience. ➤ Makes conscience effort to learn new things from home culture school even if students are generally less advanced. ➤ Is humble in attitude and willing to make mistakes. ➤ Realizes there are highly intelligent students in both cultures.	
Professional Preparation	➤ De-skilled and unprepared for re-entry into profession. ➤ Unable to admit that there are areas where TCP has become de-skilled. ➤ Unwilling to retrain or take pre/post-entry. ➤ Realizes s/he is lacking in areas but fearful of changes. ➤ Feels overwhelmed with all the changes of returning to home culture so cannot begin retraining.	➤ Realizes the need for retraining. ➤ Looking for opportunities for retraining. ➤ Takes short courses or seminar type training. ➤ Looks for new areas to expand in professionally.	➤ Is enjoying new opportunities for professional growth. ➤ Finds collegial support in training or educational opportunities. ➤ Is creative in looking at situations "outside of the box." ➤ Refuses to feel discouraged as a result of missed opportunities in home culture.	➤ Uses TCP experience as professional capital to inform new opportunities. ➤ Willing to take any job while at the same time retraining and preparing for new professional opportunities. ➤ Maintains positive attitude even though s/he may have experienced being passed over for promotions.	

TCP Re-entry Preparation Assessment

	LIMITED COMPETENCIES 1	DEVELOPING COMPETENCIES 2	PROFICIENT COMPETENCIES 3	ADVANCED COMPETENCIES 4	SCORE
Social Preparation	Record your experiences here:	Record your experiences here and celebrate your growth and development:	Record your experiences here and celebrate your proficient success:	Record your experiences here and celebrate your advanced successes:	
Academic Preparation					
Professional Preparation					

32

TCP Re-entry Preparation Reflection

Identify Where You Are on the Rubric	Highlight the phrases/descriptors that best describe your current experience in the rubric. Which column do the majority of your highlighted phrases fall into? This suggests where you are on the Re-entry Preparation Reacculturation continuum.
Write About Your Experiences	Write about a recent experience you've had that reflects lack of preparation for re-entry in some area of your life.
Apply Your Knowledge	Apply: What strengths do you bring from your background for re-entry preparation? What weaknesses do you need to be aware of?
Next Steps	What are your **next steps** to address the stressors or liabilities you are currently experiencing? List below:

33

General Overview of Timeline for Reacculturation

1 Year	2 Years	3 Years	3+ Years
➢ Beginning stages of reacculturation. ➢ A good time to stop and take stock of progress in each area. ➢ Evaluate progress and decide which areas should receive more attention. ➢ Realize reacculturation is a lengthy process and it takes time and effort.	➢ Review personal progress of reacculturation process and notice development since the one-year mark. ➢ Take specific steps to shore up areas of difficulty. ➢ Ask accountability partners to help keep reacculturation process on track. ➢ Note vulnerable areas where TCP feels like s/he is threatened and address each area with realistic goals. ➢ Note any areas of "fossilization" and begin to challenge them.	➢ Three years seems to be a stabilizing point in the readjustment process. ➢ TCPs have had opportunity to learn the ropes of a new job, regain family relationships, resettle in the community, and resume cultural competency. ➢ TCPs have had opportunity to invest social capital wisely. ➢ TCPs are generally beginning to feel stabilized in relationships as well as in productivity. ➢ A sense of self-efficacy concerning reacculturation competencies has developed or is developing in most areas. ➢ Has noted and challenged areas of fossilization.	➢ For some TCPs it may take longer than three years to accomplish full reacculturation competencies. ➢ Reacculturation goals may not be complete in any one of the areas mentioned but a lag noticed in an area should now be met with a purposeful goal. ➢ It would be wise to seek a counselor to prioritize efforts in lagging area(s) in order not to stagnate/fossilize. ➢ Keep in mind that change and growth are healthy if managed wisely. ➢ All people experience life-long change/growth. ➢ A prepared mind is able to take positive advantage of growth opportunities throughout life.
Explain your progress in year 1:	**Explain your progress in year 2:**	**Explain your progress in year 3:**	**Explain your progress in year 3+:**

34

Add Personal Meaning for your Reacculturation Transition Based on Your Rubric Scoring Results

1-point scores/ Overall score of 16–27	2-point scores/ Overall score of 28–39	3-point scores/ Overall score of 40–51	4-point scores/ Overall score of 52–64
➢ Might indicate a degree of fossilization in a specific area or areas. ➢ Fossilization implies that the reacculturation process has stopped at a specific point in a given area. ➢ TCP needs help in specific areas (e.g., language development, job training, relationship building) in order to move forward. ➢ Needs a mentor/accountability group.	➢ The TCP is moving forward in attempting to become adept at functioning in home culture after TCP experience. ➢ Fossilization is probable if positive progress does not continue. ➢ TCP stagnates in an area. ➢ This is a normal stage to pass through…but the key is to pass through the stage and to not remain in the stage.	➢ Suggests that adequacy has been reached in a specific area or areas. ➢ It is possible to reach a developmentally adequate range in one area and lag behind in another area. ➢ There is still room for growth in the reacculturation process. ➢ The TCP is able to identify areas of strengths and weaknesses.	➢ At this stage of development, the TCP experience serves as an important completion of a positive sense-of-self. ➢ Aspects of the TCP experience serve to enhance the TCP's life w/o controlling his/her life. ➢ The TCP is successful at pinpointing strengths and weaknesses and adjusts accordingly.
Add your *reflection* on your score at this time.	Add *reflections* on your score at this time.	Add *reflections* on your score at this time.	Add *reflections* on your score at this time. Take time to Celebrate!
List steps to progress:	List steps to progress:	List steps to progress:	List steps to progress:

Revisit Your Transition Journey Continuum Stages and Enjoy Your Success

Stage 1: My Current Life of Healthy Acculturation in My Host Culture	Stage 2: Forward Look at Possibilities for Reacculturation and Transition Growth	Stage 3: Active Steps for Reacculturation in My New Culture	Stage 4: Self-Assess Reacculturation Progress
1. Full involvement: make an honest appraisal of your full involvement in your current host or home community.	2. Take a forward look at Reacculturation and involvement possibilities in your next host or home community prior to disengaging from your past culture.	3. Take active steps prior to making your transition to get involved in your new setting. Plan ahead for the difficult places in your reacculturation transition by discussing possible areas of *fossilization* with your family and close friends.	4. Use the Reacculturation Rubric to assess your transition progress in your new culture. *Reflect* and *Assess* often to ensure appropriate levels of reinvolvement and healthy transition progress. Take time to enjoy your progress!

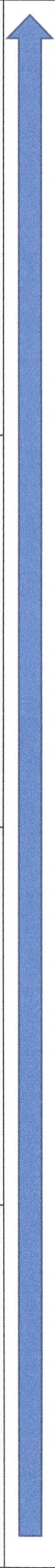

A Final Word

Dear Sojourner,

Now that you have completed your Reacculturation Cross-culture Transition reflection and assessment, take the time to enjoy your success and appreciate your journey. If you find yourself *fossilized* in an area, don't be discouraged. The first step to moving forward is to discover where you are stuck. Then continue to reflect and find steps you can take to advance further. And remember, collaboration with a friend or colleague is often very beneficial for moving forward on your journey.

If you have friends or colleagues who might also benefit from using this Reacculturation Cross-culture Transition Rubric, please share how they might obtain a copy for themselves. Successful reacculturation also means healthy cross-culture transition and is worth the time and effort to accomplish!

Your fellow sojourner,
Rachel Timmons

Acknowledgments

It is my privilege to thank so many people for making the publication of this Reacculturation Cross-culture Transition Rubric possible. First, I can honestly say that without Jo Parfitt's help and encouragement, I would not have been able to complete the publishing of this work. Her feedback, questions, and answers to my questions have directed my writing and kept me focused on completing this project. I would also like to thank Jack Scott for his design work and Paddy Hartnett for editing the draft manuscript. Their expertise and support are much appreciated.

I sincerely appreciate Ruth Van Reken and David Pollock for their pioneering work with TCKs and their books, which I often use in working with TCKs and teaching cross-culture classes. David Pollock was the first person I ever heard speak about what it means to be a Third Culture Person (when my family and I lived in Bangkok, Thailand). He presented TCK information at our church and international school, which provided excellent support for students and their families as they prepared to return to their home countries for college and work.

Tina Quick has done a fantastic job in her research, and I am incredibly thankful to Tina for using this Reacculturation Cross-culture Transition Rubric in her work with TCKs. She has been a tremendous blessing to many students and families who might have otherwise struggled through various cross-cultural issues as they transitioned between cultures.

I also extend special thanks to Tanya Crossman, Marion Knell, Erin Meyer, Melissa Chaplin, Robin Pascoe, Linda Janssen, and so many other researchers who have written books and shared resources that I continue to utilize in my professional work. Finally, I wish to thank all my students and TCKs who have been in my classes and completed research, answered questions, and conducted interviews on cross-cultural issues. You have all provided much information for this Reacculturation Cross-culture Transition Rubric, which will help many other sojourners successfully transition back to their home culture or another host culture.

Sincerely,
Rachel Timmons

Bibliography

Adler, N. J. "Re-entry: Managing cross-cultural transitions." *Group and Organization Studies* 6, no. 3 (1981) 341-356.

Austin, C. N., ed. *Cross-cultural Re-entry: A Book of Readings*. Abilene, TX: Abilene Christian University, 1986.

Cottrell, Ann. "Educational and Occupational Choices of American ATCKs." Chap.13 in *Military Brats and Other Global Nomads: Growing Up in Organization Families*, edited by Morten G. Ender. Boulder, CO: Westview Press, 2002. (This includes data comparing Third Culture Families abroad in different periods of history showing historical changes in modern third cultures.)

Hall, E.T. *Beyond culture*. Garden City, N Y: Doubleday, 1976.

Hall, E.T. *The Silent Language*. Garden City, N Y: Doubleday, 1959.

Hofstede, G. *Culture's Consequences: International Differences in Work-related Values*. Beverly Hills, CA: Sage, 1984.

Meyer, Erin. "Eight-scale Tool for Mapping Cultural Differences." *South China Morning Post* (2014). https://tinyurl.com/bzp65mww. (Culture Map.)

Oberg, K (1960). "Culture shock: Adjustment to new culture environments." *Practical Anthropology* **7** (1960): 177-182.

Pollock, David C., and Ruth E. Van Reken. *The Third Culture Kid Experience: Growing Up Among Worlds*. Yarmouth, ME: Intercultural Press, 1999.

Sussman, N.M. "The dynamic nature of cultural identity throughout cultural transitions: Why home is not so sweet." *Personality and Social Psychology Review* 4, no. 4 (2000): 355-378.

Smalley, W.A. "Culture Shock, language shock, and the shock of self-discovery." *Practical Anthropology* 10, no. 2 (1963): 49-56.

Storti, Craig. *The Art of Coming Home*. Yarmouth, ME: Intercultural Press, 2001.

Stuart, W. *What About Our Children? A handbook for MK parents, MK School personnel and missionary sending agencies*. Kandern, West Germany: IFCI Ministries, 1983.

Ting-Toomey, S. *Communicating Across Cultures*. New York: The Guilford Press, 1999.

Useem, Ruth Hill, and Ann Baker Cottrell. "Adult Third Culture Kids." In *Strangers at Home*, edited by Carolyn D. Smith, 22-35. Bayside, NY: Aletheia Publications, 1996. (This is a compilation of the five short articles that appeared in Newslinks: The Newspaper of the International Schools Service 1993-1994.)

Useem, Ruth Hill, and Richard Downie. "Third Culture Kids." *Today's Education* 65, no. 3 (1976): 103-5. (This has been reprinted in *Writing Out of Limbo: International Childhoods, Third Culture Kids and Global Nomads*, edited by Gene Bell-Villada and Nina Sichel, 18-24. Newcastle upon Tyne, UK: Cambridge Scholars Publishing, 2011.)

Ward, C., S. Bochner, and A. Furnham. *The Psychology of Culture shock*. 2nd ed. Great Britain: Routledge, 2001.

Weaver, G. R. *Culture, Communication and Conflict: Readings in Intercultural Relations*. Simon and Schuster Custom Publishing, 1996.

Werkman, S. L. "Coming Home: Adjustment of Americans to the United States After Living Abroad." In *Uprooting and Development: Dilemmas of Coping with Modernization*, edited by G.V. Coelho and P.I. Ahmed, 233-247. New York: Plenum Press, 1980.

Resources

Books

Chaplin, Melissa. *Returning Well: Your Guide to Thriving Back "Home" after Serving Cross-Culturally*. Newton Publishers, 2015.

Crossman, Tanya. *Misunderstood: The impact of growing up overseas in the 21ˢᵗ Century*. Summertime Publishing, 2016.

Janssen, Linda. *The Emotionally Resilient Expat: Engage, Adapt and Thrive Across Cultures*. Summertime Publishing, 2013.

Kohls, L. Robert. *Survival Kit for Overseas Living*. Yarmouth, ME: Nicholas Brealey, 2001.

Meyer, Erin. *The Culture Map: Decoding How People Think, Lead, and Get Things Done Across Cultures*. New York, NY: PublicAffairs, 2014.

Parfitt, Jo, and Colleen Reichrath-Smith. *A Career in Your Suitcase*. 4th ed. Summertime Publishing, 2013.

Parfitt, Jo, ed. *Forced to Fly: An Anthology of Writings That Will Make You See the Funny Side of Living Abroad*. 2nd ed. Summertime Publishing, 2012.

Pascoe, Robin. *Homeward Bound: A Spouse's Guide to Repatriation*. Expatriate Press, 2000.

Pascoe, Robin. *Raising Global Nomads: Parenting Abroad in an On-Demand World*. Expatriate press, 2006.

Pollock, David C., Ruth E. Van Reken, and Michael V. Pollock. *Third Culture Kids: Growing Up Among Worlds*. Boston Massachusetts: Nicholas Brealey Publishing, 2017.

Quick, Tina L. *The Global Nomad's Guide to University Transition*. Summertime Publishing, 2010.

Websites

Erin Meyer (Culture Mapping): https://erinmeyer.com

Families in Global Transition: https://www.figt.org

Jo Parfitt: https://www.joparfitt.com

US Department of State. "Transition, Training and the Foreign Service Child." https://2009-2017.state.gov/m/dghr/flo/c21967.htm

Van Reken's Third Culture Kids website: https://www.crossculturalkid.org

About the Author

Rachel Timmons has spent her professional life engaged in various educational and mission services in three different countries (the Philippines, Thailand, and the USA). After obtaining her bachelor's degree and teaching credential from Concordia Teachers College in Seward, NE, she taught in public and private schools in the USA and abroad. Dr. Timmons completed her master's degree from Michigan State University and a doctoral degree in Curriculum and Instruction from La Sierra University in Riverside, California.

In the course of her teaching career, Dr. Timmons served with her husband and family for 10 years at Faith Academy in the Philippines and 11 years at the International School in Bangkok, Thailand. While teaching in international schools, she had unique professional opportunities to learn from colleagues from different countries and educational backgrounds as they collaborated on developing suitable curricula for their students. She also gained much experience with teaching English as a Second Language to both children and adults. In order to be more fully equipped in this area, Dr. Timmons also earned a Certificate in Teacher of English as a Second Language.

Teaching in an international school setting provided the foundation for understanding the specific needs of international students as they learn in a language and culture different than their passport cultures. Through this international teaching and cross-cultural living experience, she became an expert in the area of cross-culture transition, especially for kids who grow up in a culture other than their passport culture or their parents' home culture. Her doctoral research examined the phenomenology of What it Means to be a Third Culture Person, which then led into the study of making healthy cross-culture transitions.

Dr. Timmons currently serves as Professor of Education at California Baptist University in Riverside, California. Out of her passion for international education, Dr. Timmons participated in developing the Master's in Education Specialization in International Education, which helps prepare teachers to serve in international schools throughout the world. She teaches classes on cross-cultural competence and has presented at conferences on various topics including Third Culture Reacculturation and Crossing Cultures with Competence. The development of this Reacculturation Cross-culture Transition Rubric flows from these years of experience and continual research in reacculturation and cross-culture transitions.

CPSIA information can be obtained
at www.ICGtesting.com
Printed in the USA
LVHW072006010422
715081LV00019B/633